ABOUT THE AUTHOR

Imogen Stirling is a Glasgow-based artist. She is a performance poet, theatre-maker, musician, writer and facilitator. She was the inaugural Writer-in-Residence for Paisley Book Festival 2021 and can be seen on BAFTA-winning Sky Arts documentary, *Life & Rhymes*, hosted by Benjamin Zephaniah. Imogen is a highly regarded artist who has performed her work widely throughout the UK and abroad (inc. BBC, Latitude Festival, Lindisfarne Festival, Aye Write, Sofar Sounds). She is best recognised for her five-star debut show, book and album *#Hypocrisy* (sell-out runs at Edinburgh Fringe and Prague Fringe; UK tour), was a participant of the BBC Words First talent development scheme (BBC Radio 1Xtra, BBC Asian Network and BBC Contains Strong Language) and she co-founded Siren Theatre Company. Imogen's work has been described as 'life-affirming artistry' (Everything Theatre), 'exactly the sort of poetry we need right now' (Alan Bissett) and 'a tonic for the tribal times we live in' (Darren McGarvey).

The live show of *Love The Sinner*, a fusion of poetry, theatre and electronic music, is currently in development.

Website: www.imogenstirling.com
Instagram: @imogenstirlingpoetry

Imogen Stirling
Love The Sinner

VERVE
POETRY PRESS
BIRMINGHAM

PUBLISHED BY VERVE POETRY PRESS
https://vervepoetrypress.com
mail@vervepoetrypress.com

All rights reserved
© 2022 Imogen Stirling

The right of Imogen Stirling to be identified as author of this work has been asserted in accordance with section 77 of the Copyright, Designs and Patents Act 1988.

No part of this work may be reproduced, stored or transmitted in any form or by any means, graphic, electronic, recorded or mechanical, without the prior written permission of the publisher.

FIRST PUBLISHED JAN 2022
REPRINTED MAY 2022

Printed and bound in the UK
by ImprintDigital, Exeter

ISBN: 978-1-913917-00-5

For everyone who has faced isolation.
For everyone who has fought for community.
We are here.
This is for you.
Thank you for opening this book.

FOREWORD

Imogen Stirling takes us through the trap doors and fire-exits of a cityscape and constraints of culture in a carafe of identities dressed as the seven deadly sins; each character is personified to perfection as she develops a narrative over an x-ray of gritty urban realism to induce a showcase of modern love.

Stirling's *Love the Sinner* asks us if anyone can control society's perception? A prescription scaled for gross reuptake inhibitors - serotonin doses to douse the masses trigger-happy to remote controls and further subscription. Asking what is behavioural and personal and what is hive mind associations in a quick-fix swift-paced rush-hour fast-food culture, we see that what is immoral becomes questionable as we delve into a deeper metamorphosis and need for a ramification of new paradigms plus less pressure to cleanse us of shame as we embody once-forbidden knowledge moving forward.

This is undoubtedly a performance piece, with parts even held in song; whilst her use of descriptive vivid language gels her to the page, her blazing theatrical style is sure to stage further success for the viewer, offering a deeper layer, a more ferocious aesthetic.

What's fascinating here is the clever intersection between the sins and the sins to their metropolis. It's beautifully cinematic as we watch Sloth as she 'blinks to free the raindrops from her lashes,' Envy likes a desk cactus as the perfect prickly prop, Greed is tech-heavy in stilettos and Gluttony is the party host, a 'conductor primed to orchestrate a night to remember.' We witness how each reacts in response due to their inherent social conditioning through Stirling's clever typecasting.

This book is about stereotypes, daguerreotypes and prototypes, the nature of relationships with self and others as genders embrace the complex beautiful mess of lives so variously speared into persona and impassioned with a poet's sensibility and a performer's flair.

Stirling's lyrical license to transcribe accelerates as it takes flight, rhythm is not just a technique, it's an actual trademark. Rivers bloat heavy, drinks overspill and yet everyone encoded by their capital vices still feels empty which leaves the reader to fill on floods of emotion and sensation from Stirling's play with words and scene set.

It's a rhapsodic account of the god-awful-gorgeousness of the blanket of sins we inhabit or adapt into our being everyday, something that honours all parties and polarities, something tagged and activated as both blessing and curse, something well worth reading.

Janette Ayachi

CONTENTS

Beginnings	13
We Meet The City	17
We Meet Sloth	19
Sloth	20
Sloth Is Forced Out The House	24
We Meet Envy	26
Envy	27
We Meet Greed	31
Greed	33
Sloth Watches The River	37
We Meet Gluttony	39
Gluttony	40
Sloth Grows Concerned About The River	43
We Meet Pride	45
Pride	46
Sloth Panics	50
We Meet Lust	53
Lust	55
We Meet Wrath	58
Wrath	59
The Crisis	66

"Jesus died for somebody's sins but not mine
Meltin' in a pot of thieves
Wild card up my sleeve
Thick heart of stone
My sins my own
They belong to me."

Patti Smith

Love The Sinner

Beginnings
18:00

Cast from the mind of a Greek,
they are seven.
Etched in memory and mauscript,
they act as guide,
warning
and legend.
Crude definitions
caught somewhere between complex and simple,
their cardinal intelligence documents
a testament of misdemeanour.
Impressive, really.
See their history and stature,
standing as pinnacles, their vision held
terrific vastness.
They span millennia
to tell us of sin.

Steadfast through time,
whittled by Christian teaching,
made media darlings.
Iconic, they shrink
as time will do.
Adjust,
as time will have.

Watch them hone.

See relics turn to roads,
tomes to tweets.

See ruins rebuild as smog-filled city
steeped in rich industrial history,
a grid plan marking harsh social divides.
Litter-lined, 9-5 grind, club strip, ashen tips,
parks and dogs and tedium.
Pavements slick with oily rainbows
dissolved in Scottish rain.
Scholars now de-robed, costumed back as vintage students,
pierced and dyed and electronic,
faces washed in android brightness.
This city
stamps its feet to shake the dust
off times gone by.

See now a city laden with expectation,
bladed with criticism.
See a city framed with billboards,
toned by filters,
see a city that blurs its rough edges.

       Our sins find themselves rough edges.

Their names softened for heavier tongues,
shortened for quicker thumbs.
Time has turned them mediocre.
Though their legends are huge, their legacies stay tiny,
compressed by the boredom of modern society.

Squint
just there -

and you might catch a glimpse of

Greed
as she smokes through pristine top-floor window,
her sighs mingle with the groans of Pride
hefting weights in the gym,
he makes the most of his lunch break. Sloth
couldn't imagine it.
She's three days deep in Netflix binge, her bedroom stale
and crisps trampled into carpet,
her mum won't like it.
Two skinny lattes and gluten-free brownies to go
at Gluttony's café, but not for him.
He's on kitchen duty, living off tips
shared by a waitress who pities him.
Trapped in her rage, Wrath
is biting her tongue
from spitting her vitriol,
Lust lies lethargic and pitiful. While Envy,
paranoia-prone and prosaic,
succumbs to Facebook inadequacy.
These moments of respite are pauses,
held breaths, commas
in the document of their immorality.

Our sins
can be found along the city's river,
a blatant reminder of nature remaining
amidst the architecture.
They walk its banks daily with
their paths never crossing,
magnets rebuffing, as it
froths and ferments with
unprecedented power.
But we'll get to that later.

For our sins
exist in urban stupor.
Alive and brutally kicking,
they stand each a phrase in the lore,
no less no more,
yet their minds twist in knots at the state of themselves
amidst it all.
Eyes of judgement are everywhere,
you cannot move for the weight of their stare.
Coddled by scrutiny, led towards betterment,
these tropes of transgression
have solid roots set into history, but today
has taught them
vulnerability.

> You'll find them drawn to the self-help shelves of
> Waterstones,
> snatching quiet minutes to seek answers in pages,
> you'll find them counting wages.
> You'll find them lost in the antisocial rabbit hole of
> Instagram,
> you'll find them buried under labels under labels under labels,
> you'll find them smothering anxiety,
> these champions of self-diagnosis
> with the number for Breathing Space saved on their phones,
> just in case.

This is a story of the seven but not solely.
For it is a story of you and it's a story of me,
it's a story of we
brought to life through aged archetypes
as they strive to fight the roles
their society prescribes.

We Meet The City
18:05

A steady soundscape settles over this reimagined city,
this Scottish city
this sinful city.

Listen to it sing the rhythms of rush hour:
    sirens, shutters, smashed glass and traffic hums,
        itchy feet,
            twitching thumbs -
                the city thrums with unrest,
                    turns a buzz of thought,
            the hours of conflict lost between
      commutes and bedtimes conduct urban angst
    now that productivity has finished
for the day.

A palette of greys, the city is bisected by a churning, bloated vein. Legend says this river once brought invulnerability, that it conceived the safety of Achilles. Legend says that promises made on its shores could not be broken, not even Zeus would be immune. Legend says that it offered a crossing to death with its passage demanding payment. Legend refashioned itself to keep up with the times with folk throwing coins and hurling chants. Its passage unpredictable, some bodies remain there still, trapped in limbo, never making it to the other side. Perhaps they lacked the coins required. These modern days, the river swells rich and viscid with trash, memories and hopes. Less focus on oaths, it snakes through this city primed with high-rises disguising poverty as progress. These modern days, the river exists as an afterthought, an attempt at nature, a hark back to the Clydebuilt vessels of industry past. These modern days, the river links our sins, maps their stories. Make no mistake, these waters are watching and these waters are changing.

  It's rained all week,
    banks bordering bursting.
      The river's close to breaking point
        and our sins stay oblivious.

We Meet Sloth
18:10

Lofty buildings line the river, housing our hero. On the heaven-scraping floor of one draughty city high-rise, windows not quite sealed at the sides, a queen amongst crumbs, seeking solace in bedsheets, Sloth pulls the blanket over her head and says *no thanks* to the rain. Snowflake by name, snowflake by nature, Sloth crowns herself the victor of stress and stagnation. Sloth chose not to vote, chose to idolise Netflix, surrendered independence to spend her late twenties sheltered by parents. Harbouring the ennui of decades of wasted energy, she stubbornly parades her failure. Inside her quilted fort, she sits atop her garbage throne, her phone screen shining bright north star. Directing her to worlds less static, more visceral, less lonely. Ignoring the sounds of life outside, Sloth welcomes a gradual slide into sleep.

Sloth
18:10

[sung]
Fell asleep watching Friends again
Saw Ross Geller's face in my dreams again
Woke up weighted with dread again
Don't have the strength to face the day again

I carried Russell Brand's book
in my backpack for days,
thumbed it fast till my fingers turned black
and the edges got frayed.
You remember the one, his Political One.
A bible to guide movement now acting
as my doorstop. But at the time
my friends and I bought it and
I know he's a twat, but something in his words
spoke to me, seemed to coax some secret
unspoken from me,
seemed to reach to a part I did not know
and he
made me feel that bit less alone, you see.

Because I try to watch the news
but I don't understand the words they say.
I don't know who they speak for, but
they don't speak for me.
I'd choose to lose myself in rom-coms
over House of Commons jargon,
but I'm told that's not useful.
Russell was preaching not to vote

and I thought that seemed excessive,
so when it came to the election I marked the
X
in the box kept for the animal welfare collective.
It made sense, that's what I think's important.
But the man next to me,
he stared at me dead,
he openly taunted
till he turned Labour red in the face,
blamed me for the downfall of our modern politics.

         IT'S YOUNG FOLK LIKE YOU!
he said

         Caught up in your pin-up's fake disillusion,
         GO DO SOMETHING THEN!
         Don't preach revolution then not follow through
         when WE fought for this, WE gave you this,
         so aim higher than your commercial messiah,
         go on then, tell me
         WHAT DO YOU WANT?

[sung]
My mind is blank but my hands ball in fists
They say us millennials are taking the piss
I watch this structure where I don't seem to fit
Don't know what I want but I don't want this

I feel the need to apologise all the time,
but I don't quite know what for.
Seems the fact I was born at the time I was born
is enough to draw scorn like breath.
So shame me, so blame me, I've heard it all before,
like how today's youth do not have the vigour to fight a war;

I don't know if that's a bad thing, perhaps we've just seen sense.
But instead we have ourselves labelled complacent.
No -
I want to get up, want to act, to find movement.
I feel it itch in my palms like the fervour of Enyo,
but it's empty avidity
because I feel like I'm wading daily through misery.
Instagram's crippling
    rent is skyrocketing
        graduates spend their days working in cafés
          because there are no jobs
            the climate is dying
              bombs terrifying
            the people are starving
        and all the while our government
    is just laughing.
See, everything's fucked!
And I am so little
and it is too late
and I'm happy just here with my bed and my crisps,
we cannot make a difference and apathy's bliss.

[sung]
The days stretch long and it's pointless to try, I feel
Life seems brighter when I close my eyes
Tell me I'm lazy, tell me what to do
I don't know where to go, but I won't follow you

Then sometimes on those 3am sleepless nights, I feel it stir.
That thing,
that some-thing,
that sung-thing,
that primal thing
that feels ancient.

That feels too big for my language to speak
but it's there like it's always been there,
it is deep.
It's there in this city's sense of community
but more, it is more.
It's transcendence of all that we think to be normal,
it's a force
propelling disciples to follow their leader, the Greeks
being swelled into riot.
It's there,
I know it's there,
it must be there,
I just don't know where to find it.

[sung]
Fell asleep watching Friends again
Saw Ross Geller's face in my dreams again
Woke up weighted with dread again
Don't have the strength to face the day

Sloth Is Forced Out The House
18:20

A sharp shriek bleep shatters Sloth's sopor, an alarm ring reminding her of places she's meant to be. A pal's house party, an empty, a promise of her presence she ought not forget. Our hero better hurry. She's been so long in four wall confines that the outside seems a dream. Elusive. A scene for other people, other lives. The day hangs like shackles from her limbs as she edges from inertia.

> *her bedroom's lost its comfort ever since the ceaseless rain*
> *saw damp patches blossom like roses*
> *they're blooming like a springtime meadow*
> *her walls moist and porous against her palms*

Needing the spur of jeopardy to push her into energy, Sloth wades through bedroom musk to meet the city's baltic kiss. The rain is slick, cloying, clamorous. Clings to you like glue. Sloth drags her heels and eyes from Tesco's dazzling glance of quick-fix snacks and blackout drinks, hauls her body to the river. This used to be her ritual, her evening pilgrimage. In the days before dread held her hand as a silent companion, she'd stand and scan the landscape. Reflect on the scenes of her grandfather's labour, spending days in the steel bellies of ships. Legacy on her doorstep. Tonight, she indulges in forgotten tradition. Watches a seagull and a crisp packet perform a ceremonial dance. Inhales the stench as thick as incense. It's manky but it's hers. It always has been.

> *the rain has filled the river to the brim*

It winds round her high-rise, has kept her occupied since

childhood, imagining what lies behind its murky horizon. She's never pinned down the way its banks conjure senses of life and death, of all that could be or be lost. Of the precariousness of it all. Of the preciousness. It holds a history she's yet to learn. When she needed answers, she would bring its gulls breadcrumb offerings and strain for prophecy in their squawks.

Shivering with raindrops dripping from half-shut lashes,
    Sloth wraps her coat around her,
        shrugs off routine passivity
            and sets forth to the party.

We Meet Envy
18:30

If Sloth were to lift her gaze, she'd spy a rolled-up scarf be hastily wedged into window cracks. A silken dam to the rain pushing through. A glossy bandage to cover a larger looming change. Too little, too late.

> *it's forming little puddles on the windowsill*
> *running down the walls*
> *sparkling warning signs, an SOS*
> *pooled reflections*
> *mirror mirror*

Sealed for now from the outside, Envy artfully places a cactus at the corner of her desk. A cup of tea. Golden. Spreads open a notebook, pages blank, an open top biro lies thoughtfully to the side. She stands on her chair to take a bird's eye photo. Swipes to Clarendon. Swipes to Gingham. overflowing with creativity, she captions. lower case. hashtag writing. hashtag evening thoughts. hashtag minimalism. hashtag life is good. The edges of her day shimmer with an emptiness she can't pinpoint, an intangible mirage bringing tears to the backs of her eyes. A sense of goals unmet, progress upset. Behind her, clothes lie draped and heaped, dirty mugs, an unmade bed. The junk kept just out of frame. The junk that we can see. Envy is an addict. Envy is beautiful. Envy is a hashtag. Envy sees through it all. But Envy wants it more than anything, Envy would give anything to be more of you and less of her. More of you and less of her.

Envy
18:30

[sung]
follow me follow me follow me follow me follow me
right to the bible of me
follow me follow me follow me follow me follow me
subscribe to the cycle of me

young girl witch birth
see her perfect
see her earn it
see her work it
save her please
life is performance
dining on laxative teas
full lips bruised knees
through the need to fit in
which is hardly a sin, is it?
hardly a sin

[sung]
follow me follow me follow me follow me follow me
right to the temple of me
follow me follow me follow me follow me follow me
get experimental with me

what's he doing
what's she wearing
where's he been
and
who's she dating

neatly captioned, sweetly angled
expert selfies in excelsis
bask
in the glow of it
bask
in the glow of its blue-lit screen approval
rabbit hole quest of edits and hues,
participant to democracy world of keyboards and touchscreens,
    obscene
veins bared daily to digital sedating
social media subscribed since age 5
    but don't undermine her, this minor is
    smarter than you'll ever be

[sung]
follow me follow me follow me follow me follow me
right to the pulpit of me
follow me follow me follow me follow me follow me
filter and sculpt it with me

she, defiant she
brushes worlds from between her teeth
strokes rites from the folds of her hair
she cleanses the history and types the old tales on her tablet
texting in tongues
one painted toe dipped in self-loathing
she knows that her world is constructed
she knows that it hangs precarious
a pretty card house in the face of tornadoes
she's the daughter of the information age
of course she knows
take her and make her your carbon copy
take her and make her your chorus mould
a slave to expectation, she craves to be

superbly normal
exquisitely mundane

[sung]
follow me follow me follow me follow me follow me
right to the prophet of me
follow me follow me follow me follow me follow me
don't somebody's daughter with me

                                      me

          me

                                                          me

me

meanwhile this city is drowning in rain
an insistent, persistent ancient threat
a message, a pre-crisis warning
reminder the planet is warming
but Envy fronts the era
of natural marketers, organic entrepreneurs
she'll take the surging river and label it tropical
she'll make you believe it all
waiting for the world to fall
not with a bang but with a tweet and flame emoji
and although she knows it
though her perfect teeth are set on edge by it
truth mars her fantasy
and closes her eyes

[sung]
follow me follow me follow me follow me follow me
right to the altar of me
follow me follow me follow me follow me follow me
lamb to the slaughter it seems

somebody's daughter, lamb to the slaughter
her selfie side-by-side
with a greenpeace caution
move attention from destruction to underage seduction
an influx of digital love
brings comfort
makes Envy
tonight
a little less empty

We Meet Greed
20:00

Let's give Envy some respite and shift across the city to focus on a workspace where notebooks and cacti have no place. Greed's desk is tech-heavy. iPhone, work phone, Macbook and iPad, all the brashness of business. 8pm and Greed is still in her office, a quick downward dog sends power through calves taut from a day of sunrise gym and sky-high heels. Outside, the streets are swarmed with pre-weekend revellers who shelter from the rain under oversized umbrellas, discarded unwanted outside bars. Inside, buckets punctuate office corridors to catch the drips, the rain is ruthless, breaking in. Uncontained leaks see the water absorbed by the carpet's tight fibres. A part of the fabric. Greed hastily removes her stilettos. No matter the façade this city attempts, to her the cracks are always evident.

> *Greed's yoga turns to squats*
> *and with each dip the river pulses*
> *with each dip, the lights begin to flicker*
> *a steady hornet buzz*
> *a threat of the outdoors taking over*

She wouldn't notice. Her mornings are Uber rides, straight through the heart of the city, no pauses in nature for her. The most greenery she sees is the front of house pot plant collection. Greed is first in, last out, you know the sort. Glass-front hubs, security codes, reception desks. Espresso and cigarette breakfasts. Lanyards and Filofax. She worships a large Malbec at her desk to fuzz the edges of a head wired from the day's rat race competition. Her acrylics snap through Twitter. Keeps it concise, stalks her city's hashtag. Once upon a time Greed did not like being from #here but now Greed calls herself from #here because Greed likes the way that #here looks now compared to how it used to. There's more to #here than high-rises and low hopes. #here shows a glossy veneer of craft beer, record shops and artisan sandwich bars. High street stores still damp from the morning's greenwashing. More like it. She likes it. She'll pass you the bucket and mop.

Greed
20:00

Once heralded The Murder Capital of Europe (!)
Obesity Centre (!)
Time to upset the titles and rewrite the narrative
with gentrification.
Not on our watch,
not if Pret a Manger has a say.

    40,000 children living in poverty

The city's hidden secrets are threatening its Commonwealth prowess,
its cultural status.
Downgrade, reframe and you'll see instead that
the kids here will scare you.
She can watch them from her window,
pre-pubescent villains running hoodlum doused in boredom.
Ghosts of Greed's childhood, she sees her brothers
in their eyes, her parents in their cries.
Their teeth are broken glass,
watch them bare their shards and laugh.

[sung]
Avert your eyes, pick up the pace
You'd make no difference anyway
Rather save attention for an H&M spending
After a hard day
Hardly a sin, is it, hardly a sin, is it?
Is it? Is it?
Hardly a sin, is it?

Ties fixed so tight, they'd choke the love in you,
dull the voice in you,
skew the thought as you pay
£8 for espresso and croissant
to wash down the anti-depressants:
normalised sedatives for 9-5 addicts,
for apathy criers,
disquiet deniers.
Greed knows that hand-to-mouth living
lacks the glamour of the movies
when there's nothing in your fridge
and Instagram pics of your notebook and coffee
won't cover your rent. See,
once you've got money,
there's nothing like it.
This round's on me becomes motto of victory,
makes your heart swell with the thrill of success
and forget where you came from;
start afresh, score out the rest.
Get your foot on the ladder,
my god you are climbing.
Once you get a head for heights,
t h e   v i e w   f r o m   t h e r e ' s   s u b l i m e .

[sung]
Avert your eyes, pick up the pace
You'd make no difference anyway
Bottle it up for the sacrament of happy hour
After a hard day
Hardly a sin, is it, hardly a sin, is it?
Is it? Is it?
Hardly a sin, is it?

Squint, just there -

and you only see rooftops and not the debris.
If you squint, just there -
makes the figures on the street
look a bit less human
and a bit more trash.
We say people make us but
what people make us (?)
what people don't make it (?)
as we airbrush the streets and
romanticise the guilt away, won't look it in its face.

Greed remembers the stomach plummet day
her brother turned up to reception,
a spectre
of sallow skin and furrowed brow, eyes sharp and darting.
She hailed security, pretended not to know him.
Power hanging by a thread, she lives with the
Sword of Damocles grazing her neck
and will guard what she has earned with feral rage,
raise the blade
to whoever dares to take it.
No care that her family's stories
tell this city's history, stand rooted in legacy.
For no one is sacred in this modern world,
we'll blot them out and write new gods,
put the casual in casualty,
make them submissive and mute them on Twitter.
They've given you all, city,
what's their reward?

(sung)
Avert your eyes, pick up the pace
You'd make no difference anyway
Rather save your two quid for a Starbucks indulgence

After a hard day
Hardly a sin, is it, hardly a sin, is it?
Is it? Is it?
Hardly a sin, is it?

The streets outside are raucous, she tells herself,
the streets outside are toxic.
There's sanctuary in corporate solitude,
she tells herself.
Alone after dark in her ivory tower block,
she makes a toast to memory,
denial leaving stains
at the bottom of her
glass.

Sloth Watches The River
20:30

Discarded Starbucks cups float on the river's surface like lily pads. The tenacious rain tosses them as lost ships. Batters and bruises them, testing their cardboard strength. If only Greed could see the spoilage. Sloth is far from tidy, but she can't understand such careless clutter. The streets are dirtier than she remembers. Debris from the city's business hub. Nonchalant declarations of wealth. Intentional neglect, a gesture of status. A world within her city she doesn't recognise. She'd never thought of it like that. Our hero is learning.

> *the downpour is a torrent*
> *ragged ugly crying rain*
> *wrenched staccato*
> *beating the pavement like a drum*

But she opts to walk to the party; the rain strips her lethargy, the river will take her there directly. Sloth watches the mob of rental bike commuters treat the pavement like a Parisian boulevard. Tuned into headphones, tyres sputter in the water, not dressed for the weather. Stopping on the bridge for a photo opp. Capturing the light turning raindrops to fireflies. Commercialising the climate. Turn to the right and your phone will present a panorama of fairy-lit boat-turned-restaurant, wide banks, still waters and metropolis hint. Idyllic. Sloth realises she keeps her back to the left. Always has. No one wants to see where the city's sorrow groans at its seams. It doesn't look good on camera. This is a city of two halves, a city of a better half. A city she knows like the palm of her hand. Despite grander plans, she's never strayed far from its familiarity, hung between its two extremes and blind to both. And she loves it. Despite it all, despite the flaws, she loves it. Right down deep in her bones, she loves it. Tonight, she lets her eyes take in the whole vast wet scale of it. Blows a kiss. Continues.

We Meet Gluttony
21:00

Sloth's destination has cheap strobe lights illuminate hot breath and cigarette smoke, creating hazy trails. Prepped for the party, stomach lined and ready, tonight is Gluttony's night. He's the host, the conductor primed to orchestrate a night to remember. A night to put him on the radar. Intimidated by chaos, Gluttony is jaded but craves stimulation. Stumbling drunk on peer pressure, Gluttony is thoughtless, excessive. Exists without limits, he's a binge addict. An impulse devotee, he labels spontaneity to disguise reckless tendencies. His flat borders the river and the disco lights are a siren call to lost sailors in need of a dance. A beacon to Sloth, traipsing slowly to the gaff.

> *it's the eighth day of rain and the river looks unhealthy*
> *it lies there like a swollen belly*
> *it rumbles and moans like a wounded animal*
> *it's asking for saving*
> *put out of its misery*
> *and no one is listening*

Gluttony watches it slosh and surge like heaving bile. It turns him seasick. Midnight mould is creeping across his ceiling, fractured and leaking. The river is entering the building. The thin walls are soaking. The structure is groaning. Gluttony knows it shouldn't be so, but he turns down the lights to conceal it. Excessive by name, neglectful by nature.

Gluttony
21:00

The clock strikes evening forward on this Friday night
and the flat is rife with unfulfilled tension,
torpor and consternation.
He'd lingered at the Tesco shelves till
certainty approached. Dismissed notions
of rent, bills and kindly loans
to grab Bacardi and Coke before the spell broke.

[sung]
Hardly a sin, is it, hardly a sin?

The party's his tonight, congregated strangers
crazed by consumption, straining
to fit the given mould of student culture.
Each slightly queasy at the night's prospect, yet
drink until drink until drink until drink
until arrogance bursts forth through anxious ribs
and holds its own
in a zone of masturbatory ego stoking,
brash and unfolding. Peacocks
preaching politics and boasting philosophy,
filled to the brim with cheap mixer and gin
till collective vomiting of confidence
sets guards back up,
left
sick
with
lust
for unattainable life.

[sung]
Fill me up
I cannot get enough
Fill me up
I just want to be loved

He's crept upstairs early, nauseous and lonely
and in need of bedroom safety.
Beats bleed through walls,
but housed in blanket womb
that wound stays sutured; reclusive,
not in the mood to talk rumours.
The scene downstairs is a sea
of clashing vanities, bereft of friendship,
an empty ruse to rally
tomorrow's profile pictures.
Extending the fiction of How To Do Weekends.

> he just wants a hand to hold, an arm to slip under
> he just wants to forget the red-stamped letters
> the broken heater, the battle to make ends meet
> he wants to forget he spent her money
> on a disco strobe
> desperate for acceptance
> he wants to hate her for trying to protect him

[sung]
Hardly a sin, is it, hardly a sin?

Her waitress tips masquerading as Wi-Fi assistance
went on a litre of lime-flavoured paint stripper,
he necks it and undoes his zipper.
She said she wants the best for him,
she always wants the best for him.

Two years younger than him,
he cringes at the ridicule
of her concern.
Thoughts swim in vodka seas as he takes a clumsy picture.
Sends it to her.
A gift, he thinks.
Unsolicited.
Illicit.
Explicit.
Idiot.
Burned pupils imbued with hateful toxicity,
eyes glazed, money wasted, binged and broken.

       he thinks of the jokes that they share in the kitchen
       as she carries used plates
       and he flips her a pancake
       their cigarette breaks, their bus shelter waits
       he thinks of the way she draws a smiley face
       every time
       on the stiff brown envelopes she splits her tips into
       slips inside his bag with a nonchalant grin
       he thinks of her waking for her 6am shift
       the crime on her phone screen
       he thinks of her starting her day with his sin
       and remorse is a blade twist

[sung]
Fill me up
I cannot get enough
Fill me up
I just want to be loved

Sloth Grows Concerned About The River
21:30

Pilgrimage ended, Sloth stands at Gluttony's flat attempting to wring the rain from her hair. It hangs thick with cloudburst. At first, the downpour was refreshing, she'd felt herself again. For so long her purpose has lingered like a loose balloon. Out of reach. A lost thing. Tonight, the rain had shocked her to attention, put power in her sodden steps. But now, Sloth feels unease gnaw at her because something's not normal. She blinks to free the raindrops from her lashes then has to blink again.

> *the river hasn't stopped rising*
> *a straining squeezebox, pounding waves*
> *blink*
> *the river hasn't stopped rising*
> *people are passing*
> *and no one is noticing*
> *blink*

Gentle belches as pockets of water jump to shore and are sucked into drains. Dark puddles are seeping onto pavements and collecting in the trouser hems of businessmen. Blink, blink. A merging of elements, water venturing into earth's realm. Unnatural. Long-hidden treasures are making an entrance: a dislodged shopping trolley, someone's lost shoe. Things are being revealed. Streetlamps are flickering. Phone lines are crackling. Static is prickling. Things are breaking up. A bold wave leaps forth and seeps into Sloth's socks. At that moment –

> Envy's phone dies and her panic
> eases to peaceful vibrationless silence.

At that moment -

                Greed sings under her breath
                in the soft harsh accent of
                her brother. At that moment -

Gluttony lets himself cry
with hot stomach acid tears.
Sloth turns up her music,
tries to tune out the splashes

           At that moment - the city prepares to cast
           its phobic judgement on a ruptured Pride.
           Lust stands on the precipice of gendered
           violence. Wrath takes a breath to keep
           the demons quiet. At that moment –
           their fates rest in their hands only
           and we can do nothing but watch.

The tension shivers. The river loudens. Sloth is drowning in the pressure. Rejecting party plans she strides forward, she wants to know more, she has to see where this is going. Still, nobody is noticing. The first flash of lightning strikes like a serpent. Drivers blare their horns as they attempt to navigate deep purgatory puddles. She stumbles past the city park, the grass thick and waterlogged. She watches figures immune to it all, she sees a man sit ankle-deep in it all. Her mind spirals as she thinks how this could play out. Visions of cataclysm. Mythical destruction. She wishes herself virile to act before time runs out. Our hero's journey isn't over. There is time, she thinks, there is time.

We Meet Pride
22:50

Pan back to the city park, a civic Eden. Let's stall here a minute, take stock of the man resisting knowledge of the Fall. In the summer, this park is a riot of children and picnics and hipsters; this evening, it's quiet. Broken glass sits in mandala patterns round bins, the pigeons peck crumbs from between. A brutal, dirty beauty. This park offers refuge to the city's resurrection men. Refuelled and numbed and ready. Pride sits lonely by the river. His eyes stare empty at the depths as though to count each penny-wasted wish collected. The rain has whipped his cheeks red raw and his feet sink deep into the sodden grass.

> *the water circles his ankles like fetters*
> *he finds himself set, his feet chilled marble*
> *let him be an ancient sculpture*
> *immersed*
> *let him be consumed*

He lifts his eyes, then drops them, as a frenzied young woman runs by him.

On any given day, Pride's life reads like a Facebook highlights reel. Matinee idol, the masculine ideal. Young, fun and successful, Pride thrives on the thrill of his excellence. He has his own place in the centre of the city with treadmill and balcony, pot plants and potpourri. Golden boy, the great achiever; perceived as the bravest and boldest, we find Pride at his lowest. Pride has faced an ego drop that's left him feeling hopeless. Recoiled from his own definition, his vision turned murky as the water's surface. His image deflated, Pride thinks he is nothing without his reputation.

Pride
22:50

He woke up and there was peace,
like a perfect vacuum.
Horizontal in a room that smelt of space,
that brought him grace
from usual daily mornings laced with friction.
Her body tensed with frosted animosity
that he attempts to melt with puns and coffee vapours
as they sit in breakfast table stalemate,
conversation long evaporated
into disinterest.
She is a heavenly statue, cold and
impassive.
The house hangs heavy on her word –
but not today.
This morning brought forgotten respite,
eased into the day
with open heart and gentle wake,
just his arm
draped tender
over
his waist.

Pride is Man.
Sweet routine of morning run and night-time gym,
exfoliate for perfect skin then beers to rough it up again.
Grad job, new wheels and FIFA on Sundays,
he plays the role perfectly, down to a tee.
They see him a modern Adonis,
all carpe diem and signature flawless.

They see him a modern Man,
all techno and dick jokes.
His girlfriend is beautiful, they make quite the pair.
She's the talk of the office,
'golden'
they call them,
all couple goals hashtags.
It makes him feel smug, it defines him.
Tries to keep this in mind
as the boredom starts biting,
the interest starts dying,
he sees her eyes wandering
and they argue more than they talk.
And though he's not really that bothered,
he holds on to her still like a crucifix.

Because he is Man
and this morning's duvet clings to the blood
of punctured ego, it's gooped and sticky,
holds him down like a fist.
This room looks different to him,
the same space
where they've smoked
and they've talked
and they've studied
and laughed
for as long as he's known,
his best friend, his gaff.
Now it looks like a trap, now he looks
like a bad decision. Always so easy
in his skin;
he sees him now still slick with midnight sweat
and cheeks flushed rose
with baby blush, what is he dreaming of?

Adam and Adam,
they lay tight, ribcages pressed
with umbilical closeness.
He makes him think poetry.
He is Man,
he is Man,
is he Man, when
nothing even happened,
they just talked and fell asleep, he was so kind,
you see. She'd locked him out their place again,
refused to see his face
again.
He bought them beers, he rolled a spliff,
he listened.
Pride can't remember the last time
that somebody just listened.

But he is Man
and everywhere he looks now
everything seems phallic,
everywhere he looks, it feels like
someone's laughing.
They are stone-carved god men
moulded through history
to be what they are today.
They are Strong Men, Hard Men, Tough Men
yet everything's fragile,
one step out of line and identity's shattered,
all they have worked to maintain.
Pride has rainbows coursing through his veins
and he feels shame
and he feels clarity
and the river is staggering,
certain to break any moment.

He should cry out
but his throat is choked with words of love
and hate and loneliness.
So all he can do is
hiss through his teeth at him
as he blinks the day awake.
And spit at his goodness while his stomach
twists at the thought
of the guys at work
and the girl at home
and their words
and their looks
and he's scared
and he's sick
and he just wants
to hold him.

Sloth Panics
23:10

Pride's cluttered thoughts are hushed by a grumbling coming from the river depths with volcanic threat. Clouds have gathered dense as knotted brows and the rain falls like a sheet. There is no reprieve. Car alarms wail as they are tipped onto their sides, the pavements are running streams. Power lines crackle and streetlights die. Bins overflow with the water. Bikes bounce in the shallows. Posters stripped from walls turn balls of branded mulch and bob like buoys atop the flood. Sloth holds back hysteria at the farce of it all. She watches Pride sit now shin-deep in water, sees him drop his head and shut his mind to the biblical risk at his feet, and it turns her. All the longing of those 3am sleepless nights for that thing

      that primal ancient thing

           that eye-opening

world-shattering

             alive-and-kicking

    thing

burns in her. Her flesh is alight with it. A flame so fresh and fundamental, she feels it. From deep within herself, she finds it. Sloth rips her music from her ears and runs with a fury she forgot she possessed. Her feet

slip on bursting gutters as she shouts for people to run!
For people to look at the water! For people to panic!
And look up! And see! What is happening! Right in
front of their eyes! They stare past her as another of the
city's eccentrics and go about their evenings avoiding
the oracle unbolted from lethargy to place herself
between them and the urban surf. They ignore her,
they look by her and she feels a duty handed to her.
Our hero, in action.

Sloth fixes her gaze on the river that's followed her
life, unbiased. With radical stance, she plants herself as
shield, willing herself to command its retreat, willing
to swear an unbreakable oath to force its submission.
Channelling Greek solemnity, accepting celestial
consequence. Summoning memory she sees herself

> stand on its shore every night
> she hears the stories she's spun it
> of plans for action
> for hope
> for uprising
> for change

Her vows had seemed shrill and young, but the river
had listened. She remembers the way it inspired her,
she remembers how apathy drenched her. She looks
at the river, eyes fixed and steady, and swears she will
do it again, she will try it again, she swears she will not
give up hope again. Sloths asks the river to surrender
its power. She asks the river to lend her its power. She
feels its rampant rage alive in her veins and suddenly
she is the water, she asks the river if it wants her. She is
willing to give herself in exchange for it stopping, she

plunges her arms deep into its body and waits for its answer. Her chest beats for her city and all of its kindness and all of its people and all of their blindness and she waits. Rebirthed, renewed, resplendent, our hero waits with fear and she waits with love.

The city vibrates with her change.

We Meet Lust
23:40

Elsewhere, Lust learned about love through the internet. With the calculated heed of a mathematics student, he consumed angles and figures, curves and positions. One over two equals halfway to something. Three over one equals top evening viewing: *rough love with young lust / whole day loving / real amateur love / fit lust destroys love next door / use me for a quick love.*

The sky outside is dark, air humming with an energy like something's got to give. Like Judgement Day. There's violence in the sky. Heavens pregnant with the threat of thunder, as lightning zigzags knife stabs. Lust languishes in a power cut, unsettled on the edge of his bed.

> *the rain battering like bullets isn't helping*
> *they've cracked his windowpanes*
> *formed fragile fractals*
> *raindrops creeping through like blood*
> *like tears*
> *making puddles on his floor*

Lust loves his girlfriend when she blows him, feels an absence when she holds him. Lonesome. Her sadness sand-trickles through his stiff computer fingers. He can never quite grasp her. Lust knows to grow stronger, bigger, harder, seeks to feed an insatiable hunger. He wants more than she can give him, seeks to push her past her limits. A guilt tugs at him. Makes him turn his phone over when he sees her name, keeps his eyes glued to the screen. Seared into his retinas, nightly routine. The room reverberates from the door she slammed behind her. Lust cannot think of his behaviour, what he did to her, so he trains his brain to the pulsating in and out and in and out of the figures on the screen. With every thrust, the river gains strength. With every push of hate, the river gags. The river is approaching climax.

Lust
23:40

[sung]
Teach me, show me
Love me, hold me
Take me far from being lonely
Teach me
Love me
Take me, take me, take me lonely

Lust loves her too much.
Thrusts devotion down her throat
until she spills sonnets.
He wants it, he wants it,
he wants it.
Locked in his bedroom watching
rough yearning,
learning
the way to a woman's heart is
through hurting.
Rehearsing the sermon, preaching
contortion,
reframing.
Removing the shame in
loving through pain.

[sung]
Hardly a sin, is it, hardly a sin?

Lust loves love.

Loves to un-see and reconstruct
reality to feed his
simulated expectation. See him
proclaim and praise his angel till the day
he snaps her halo
when she slips from captive pedestal.
Impossible.
He tried so hard, he tried to love,
he dressed his heart in ropes and cuffs,
he offered roses dipped in blood,
Lust tried to keep a grasp of love.

[sung]
Teach me, teach me

He'd pushed her, oh he'd pushed her.
In an act of desperation, body shaking,
icy sweat. He needed the hit
of fantasy fulfilled,
he needed it.
He'd felt himself a circus beast preparing
for the flaming
hoops of masculinity, addicted to the game.
He'd pushed her, wanted her to know
that he could roar
louder than her fear.
He had pushed her,
he had trapped her,
he had hurt her
with the unspeakable.
Now the silence between them sits solid as a grave.

[sung]
Hardly a sin, is it, hardly a sin?

Lost in the depths but he didn't know better.
Spoon-fed obscenities through
digital wet dreams.
Child seeks love in a time of misogyny,
lust in an age of monogamy.
Tendrils of shame sprout weed-like
in his chest but are matchless against
a heart that is senseless.
Instead his mind shifts from regret to how to find
his next conquest.
Lust lays
sprawled across bedsheet
in prostrate reverie, he
collects tears in crumpled tissues,
lines the bin with his misuse.

[sung]
Teach me, show me
Love me, hold me
Take me far from being lonely
Teach me
Love me
Hardly a sin, is it, hardly a sin?

We Meet Wrath
23:55

Across the hall from Lust, our final figure brews chamomile concoctions to soothe a racing mind. The tiniest tonic to the outrage outside. The block has been shocked into darkness by the storm, candles trace a path through this flat. Hunting for moments of quiet, moments of still, Wrath is an accidental night owl. Her chest-tight nights summon sleep to silence the loop of chatter, incessant and endless. Running on repeat like a subway line. High blood pressure, fidgeting, tempers. Symptoms of the senseless quest for better, for betterment, this veteran of self-help quests manifesting in unrest. Edgy, tense, a temperamental powder keg. An expert at composure, Wrath knows how to dampen her anger and present serenity. The world sees her calmness, while she has herself walking on eggshells and swallowing words, keeping her censored. Wrath lies on her bed. Wrath closes her eyes.

> *Wrath's room is raining*
> *a fine mist has pushed through thick tenement walls*
> *and turned to drizzle*
> *the air is alive with it, the walls are slick with it*
> *the explosion of the rain outside makes*
> *Wrath feel like the eye of the storm*
> *sheltered by an anger*
> *larger than her own*

Full fat drops are bouncing onto Wrath's face. And while she should be unnerved, she feels the first genuine smile of the day as she lets it wash the rage away.

Wrath
23:55

Wake up early, rise with the sun,
don't snooze, don't lie in.
          Lie in.
Get a full eight hours,
ten hours, nine -
make like the Spanish.
Meditate:
every day, twice a day,
when you wake,
never more than once a week.
Appreciate,
list five things you are grateful for,
manifest, set intentions.
Cleanse, tone,
apply: serum, eye cream, moisturise, oil up, sunscreen,
hydrate, prime, sculpt your brows, dress your eyes.
Apply: foundation, concealer, bronze, blush, highlight.
Lips
          Lips
                    Lips
Powder and spray.
Don't take too long on your appearance,
don't think too much of your appearance,
don't try too hard.
          Be natural
in twelve easy steps.
Dress up, dress down,

wear heels, wear flats.
It's hot outside (don't show skin)
It's hot outside (show skin)
Not too much skin -
it's hot.
Skip breakfast, never skip breakfast.
Fast
intermittently
Eat
not too much.
Don't eat too much.
Have one black coffee -
Good For The Heart.
Avoid caffeine -
Bad For The Heart.
Eat fruit, don't eat fruit
before 11,
it's high in sugar.
Drink water,
juice everything.
Yoga   run   stretch   move
Don't exercise too soon after eating.
Don't *don't*
don't do it like that.

[sung]
Don't, don't, don't do it like that
Don't, don't, don't do it like that
Don't do it, don't do it
Like that
Don't, don't, don't do it like that

Wrath can't understand why she's angry all the time.

She works.
Work, work, work, work, work
for the wage, for the passion, for prestige,
for the women.
Care about money, don't care about money,
it's progressive, *it's vulgar.*
Procrastinate! It's healthy.
Don't procrastinate! It's lazy.
TEN LIFE HACKS YOU NEVER KNEW EXISTED!
To make life better,
to make you better,
make you better, make you better, make you better, make you
increase productivity,
meet your deadlines,
update socials on your lunch break,
do yoga on your lunch break.
Don't take your work home.
Don't, don't, don't.
Have a four-day week.
Have a work/life balance.
Meet your deadlines,
meet your deadlines.
Laugh off the colleagues who hit on you,
the boss who patronises you,
the city streets that see you as fair game,
as prey.
Put that away and
cycle home
     get fresh air
          ignore the catcalls
Don't talk loud,
don't take up space,
take up space.
Be a Boss Bitch,

be a feminist,
don't be a feminist,
don't call yourself a feminist.

[sung]
Don't, don't, don't do it like that
Don't, don't, don't do it like that
Don't do it, don't do it
Like that
Don't, don't, don't do it like that

Wrath can't understand why she's angry all the time.

Be independent!
Go out alone!
Don't go out alone!
Don't walk home alone!
Text me when you get home!
Don't wear headphones!
Don't leave your drink!
Don't think you're safe!
Don't sleep with him!
Don't dress like that!
Don't entice him!
Don't entice him!
fill your lips, fill your tits, fill your face, lose your lines
Don't entice him!
Don't, don't, don't.
Act your age, don't look your age.
Don't try too hard!
Don't get raped!
Relax.

Wind down, have a bath.

Practice self-care (in a feminist way).
One large Merlot,
absolutely no booze.
Do not use your gadgets,
screen are bad,
Netflix, no chill.
Drink tea,
no caffeine after 7.
Meditate.
Meditate.
Count your breaths.
Listen to your breaths.
Listen to music.
Listen to nothing.
Read a book.
Have a snack.
Don't eat.
Remove your makeup,
never sleep in your makeup,
never let a man see you without your makeup.
Cleanse, eye cream, tone,
serum, retinol,
moisturise,
face oil.
Perfect sleep in seven simple steps.
Set – *don't set* - an alarm.
Sleep
peacefully.

[sung]
Wrath can't understand why she's angry all the time
Wrath can't understand why she's angry all the time
Why she's angry all the time
Why she's angry all the time

Angry all the time

Wrath tries so hard not to step outside the lines
but she's angry all the time, all
the time,
all the time.
Wrath laughs at the rain forcing into her space,
Wrath opens the window, welcomes cascade,
she laughs.
Wrath watches a woman run mad through the street
shouting in the faces of men.
She laughs, a Boudica bellow.
The city's a cesspit of
patriarchal bullshit, poster feminists;
bosses whose throwaway comments
tying blowjobs to promotions
are forgotten in a moment
but sit with you like ghosts,
they haunt you.
Midnight is approaching, the witching hour.
The strength of nearly-burned women
propelling into morning. The pain of this history
clamps Wrath like an ankle tag and
at that moment
she understands why she's angry all the time.

Wrath greets her anger
and with the force of the women they tried to eradicate,
Wrath screams a farewell to control and restraint.
Her vocals a chorus of decades of frustration:
she screams
she *screams*

and every window in the city shatters.

The rain turns to diamond shards of falling glass
and for a moment
all the city's sinners become sparkling silhouettes,
they are everywhere.
You can see them on the streets, bright at empty window frames.
The city is lit with their glittering fragility.
And Sloth, with the valour of a martyr,
throws herself into the river.

The Crisis
00:00

The banks break.

The water roars.

The freezing river hits Sloth

at full force.

She finds herself knocked to her back and closes her eyes to imagine what surrender will feel like. And while the panic howls, there's a solace at its heart because Sloth knows that she tried. Her vision is clearer than she can remember. Our hero. Awake. Her age-old roots clasp hands with modern compassion and she feels herself shaken from hibernation.

She opens her eyes a slit and as she
squints, *just there*, through the water

>she sees Envy stare her careful fantasy square in the face,
>she sees her accept it, she sees her reject it.
>She sees Greed turn down the taxi and walk the streets,
>learning the city behind the pretence.
>Gluttony vows to recognise kindness,
>Pride smiles as he recollects tenderness,
>Lust comprehends emptiness.
>Wrath stands on a bedroom stage of icy water
>and broken glass,
>yells and yells and revels in the thrill.
>Sloth sends them love.

> Wherever their stories take them, she wishes them love.
> Whatever this crisis might change, she wishes them hope.
> Sloth and her river might not be their saviour
> but at least they can be an awakener.

The river vomits its load. Trash is spewed everywhere. Sloth is propelled back onto shore and with the air punched from her lungs, she sees faeces mixed with coins. Shopping bags, jewellery, phones. A trainer. A broken umbrella. The city's ugly treasures. Exposed. Vulnerable. Revived.

> And then it retreats,
> as quickly as it came,
> the purge is done,
> the cleanse has come.

Left behind is a patchwork display of goods, grotesquely intimate. Sloth sits amongst it, all wet denim and heavy breath. She is soaked. *Is that all it was?* Her heart is a hammering frantic fist.

Somewhere in the city, a clock chimes midnight.

A seagull screams. Pedestrians walk. A girl laughs. Nothing has changed but something has loosened. A collective sigh. A crisis quietened. Sloth sits up and laughs at the passing. She SHOUTS with a voice too long suppressed by media doom diets and social assumptions. She SHOUTS at the river to thank it for its warning. She SHOUTS at the river to thank it for its power. She feels the hope settle in her, she feels the sin ebb from her and somehow, some way, she thinks of the others.

Somewhere inside her

> she understands Greed's heartache
> and prays that it turns to acceptance.
> She yearns that Envy knows confidence,
> she wishes Pride a journey
> and a quiet strength for Gluttony.
> Knows each can learn revelation should they earn vindication.
> Her jaw clenches for Lust but she trusts he knows togetherness.
> Wrath glows with empowerment
> and Sloth hopes it withstands.

They are each too far gone to be undone, no fixing but cleansing. Unburdened, offered a shot at freshness.

Dear sinners,
embrace it.

Sloth bathes in ancestral knowledge and sees that, cast from the mind of a Greek, all seven are kintsugi creations, crafted of golden scar and candid despondency. They drive their stories through a city that dangles acceptance just out of reach, like distant moons. Earnest and futile. She sees the seven stand as fallen angels with their halos at an angle. She sees them guilelessly become the story of all people. After all, this was a story of you and me. Of we. Sloth sees us laden with the weight of innocence and guilt that always has existed and understands that we are myth and we are modern. We are legend and we are human. Story and truthful. And sinful? Oh yes. Fallible and beautiful.

ACKNOWLEDGEMENTS

With thanks to my dramaturg and friend Luke Holbrook for your guidance and provocations throughout the development of this piece.

Thanks also to Sarah, Jack, Michael, Adam, Simone and Emi for your musical sensitivities and flair.

Thank you to Creative Scotland for funding the creation of the script and music, allowing me to work alongside such brilliant artists.

The warmest gratitude goes to my wonderful family and to Jason for your steadfast support and kindness throughout the writing process. Always, but especially when the world came to a standstill. Thank you.

ABOUT VERVE POETRY PRESS

Verve Poetry Press is a quite new and already award-winning press that focused initially on meeting a local need in Birmingham - a need for the vibrant poetry scene here in Brum to find a way to present itself to the poetry world via publication. Co-founded by Stuart Bartholomew and Amerah Saleh, it now publishes poets from all corners of the UK - poets that speak to the city's varied and energetic qualities and will contribute to its many poetic stories.

Added to this is a colourful pamphlet series, many featuring poets who have performed at our sister festival - and a poetry show series which captures the magic of longer poetry performance pieces by festival alumni such as Polarbear, Matt Abbott and Genevieve Carver.

The press has been voted Most Innovative Publisher at the Saboteur Awards, and has won the Publisher's Award for Poetry Pamphlets at the Michael Marks Awards.

Like the festival, we strive to think about poetry in inclusive ways and embrace the multiplicity of approaches towards this glorious art.

www.vervepoetrypress.com
@VervePoetryPres
mail@vervepoetrypress.com